I0829357
BPD
Relatable Thoughts
Coloring Book

I Hate You-
Don't Leave
Me!

I think about dying but I don't want to die.

Be
gentle with
yourself.

destructive!

I'm scared to
get close,
I hate
being alone.

I have a
lot of
hatred
for myself
but a lot of
love
to give.

These feelings will pass, they always do.

I'm trying my hardest not to act how I feel.

You say it's all
in my head .....
I know
and it's a real
issue.

I need to
be sure
you
are okay.

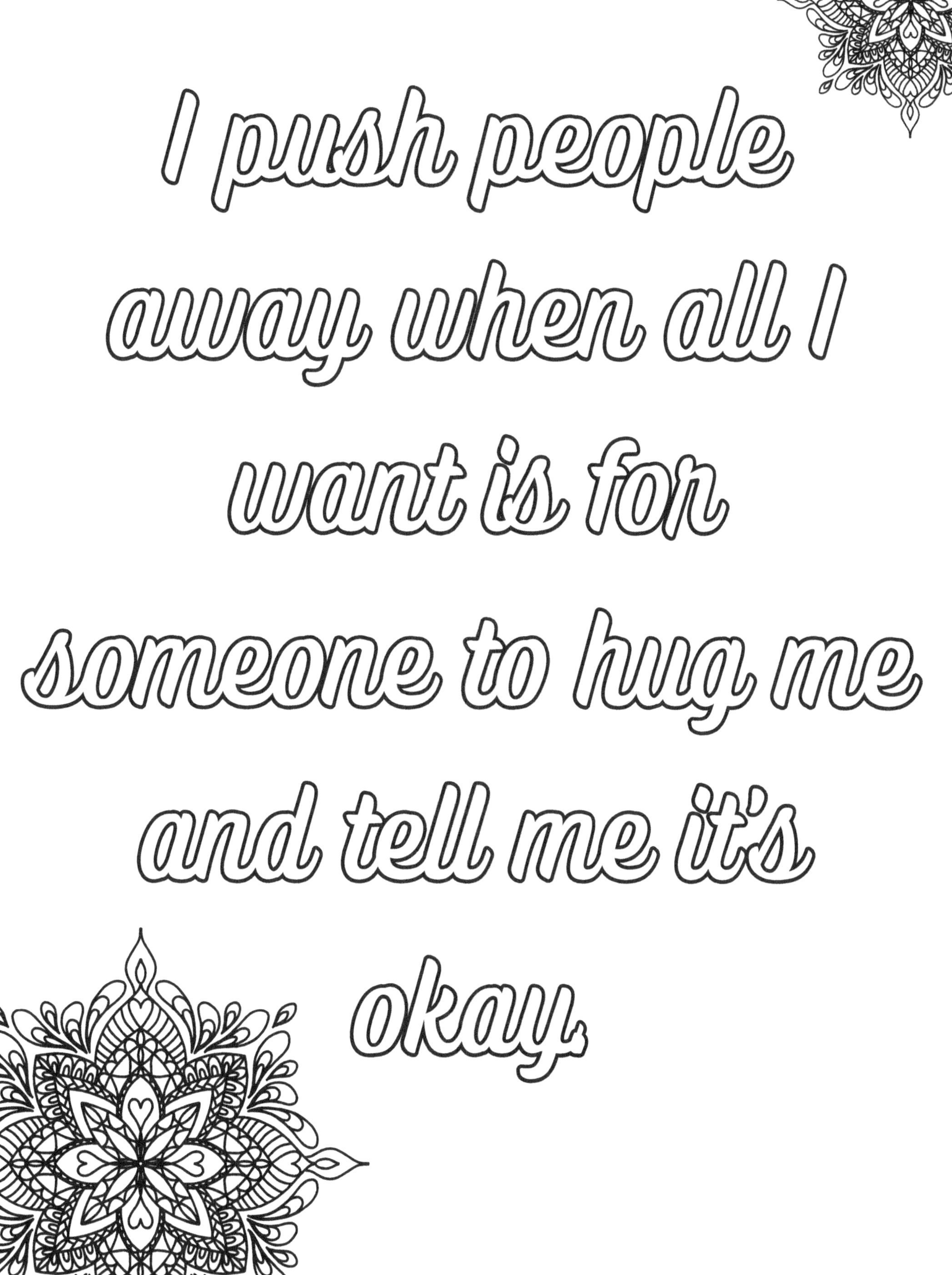
I push people away when all I want is for someone to hug me and tell me it's okay.

Just because I carry it well, don't think it isn't heavy.

I don't
always jump,
but when I do
it's to
conclusions!

Different

I'm happy,
but
I'm sad.

I feel everything... All the time!

Too worn out to socialize.

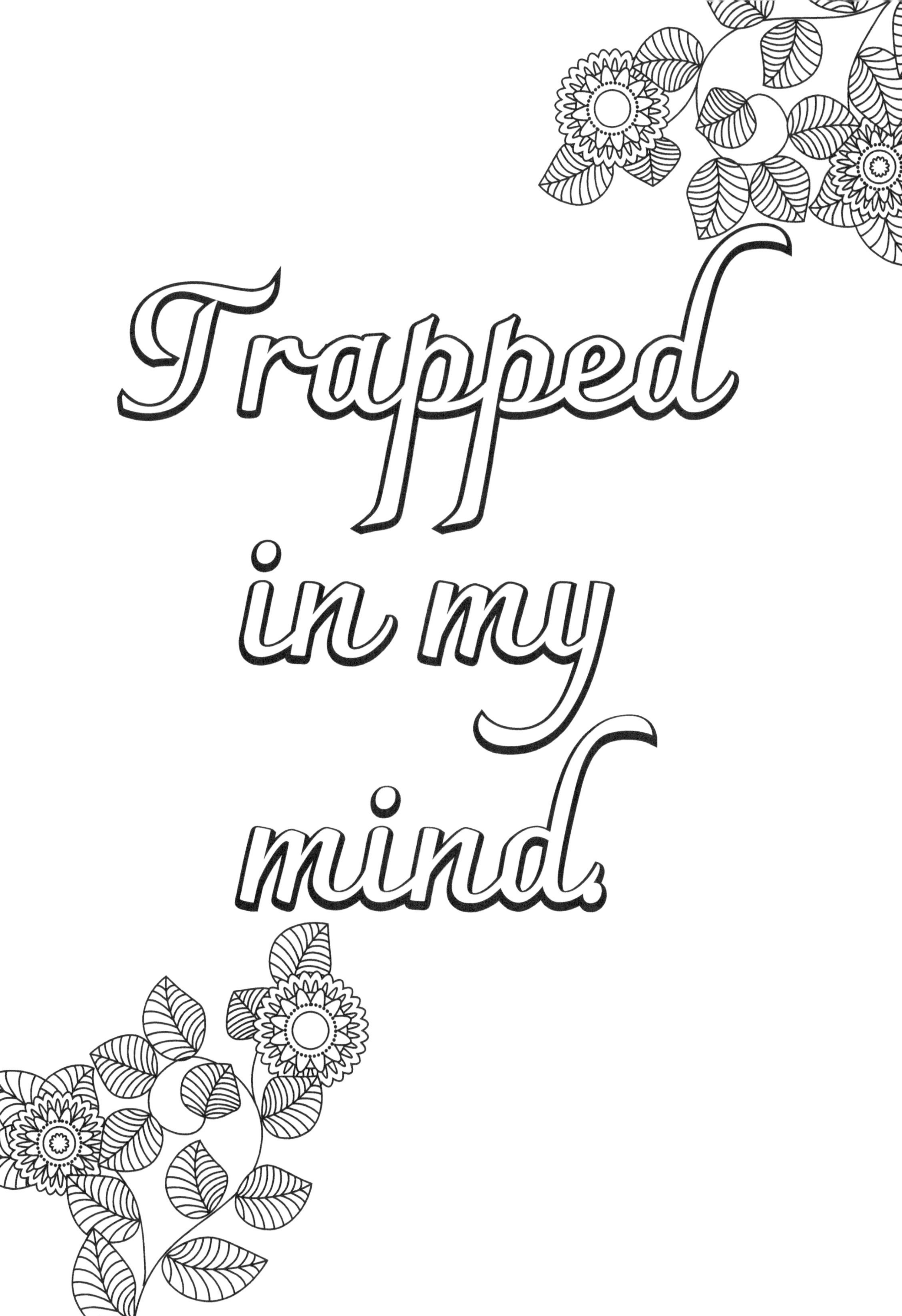

Trapped
in my
mind.

Breathe!

Just because
I carry it well,
don't think
it isn't heavy.

I endured
childhood trauma
and all I got
was this
personality disorder.

Am I allowed to be upset or am I being oversensitive?

I pretend
to
fit in,
I rarely do.

How does it
feel
to not
feel it ALL?

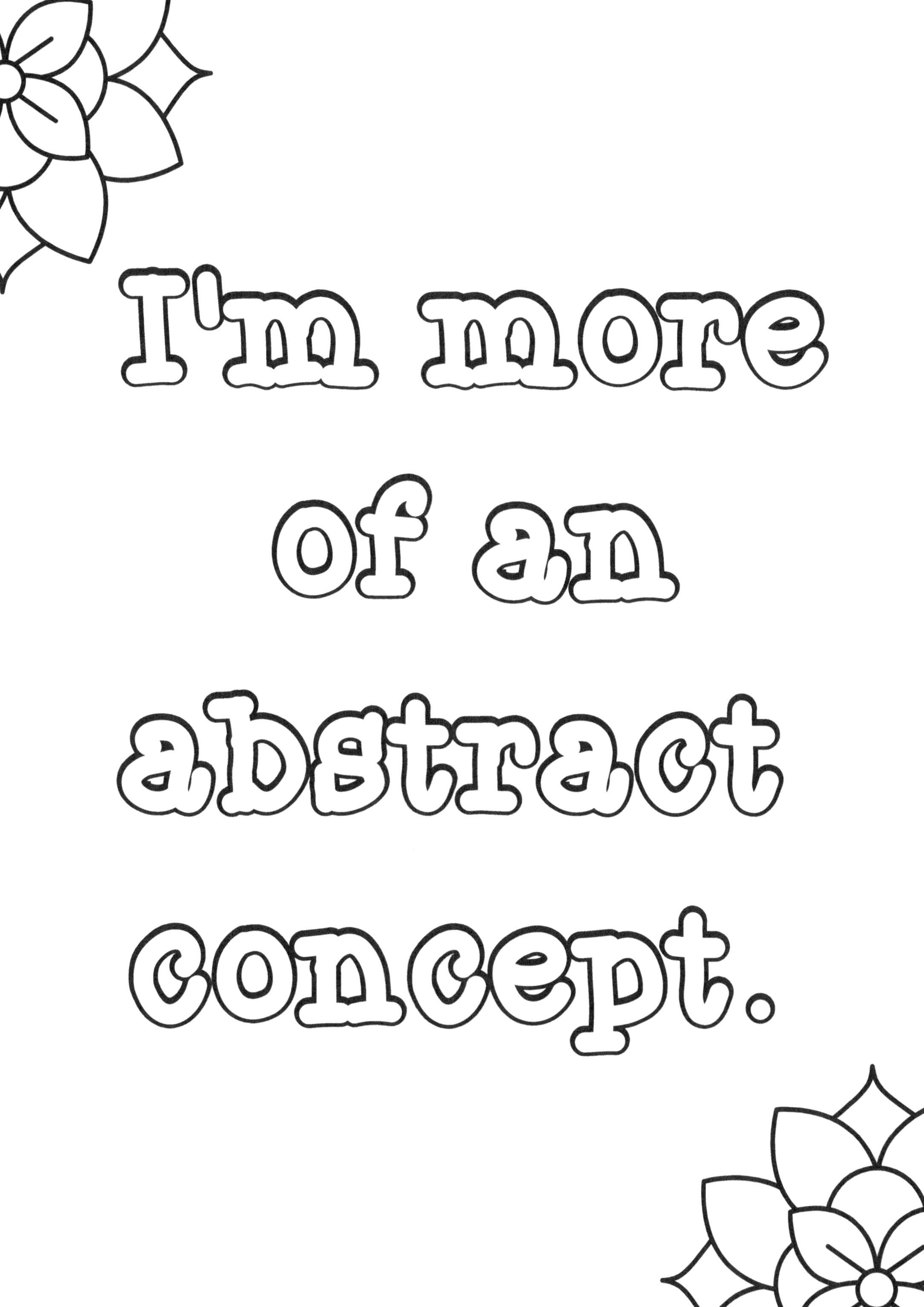

I'm more
of an
abstract
concept.

You are brave,
capable, and
significant.

I isolate myself, but I hate to be lonely.

Frantic

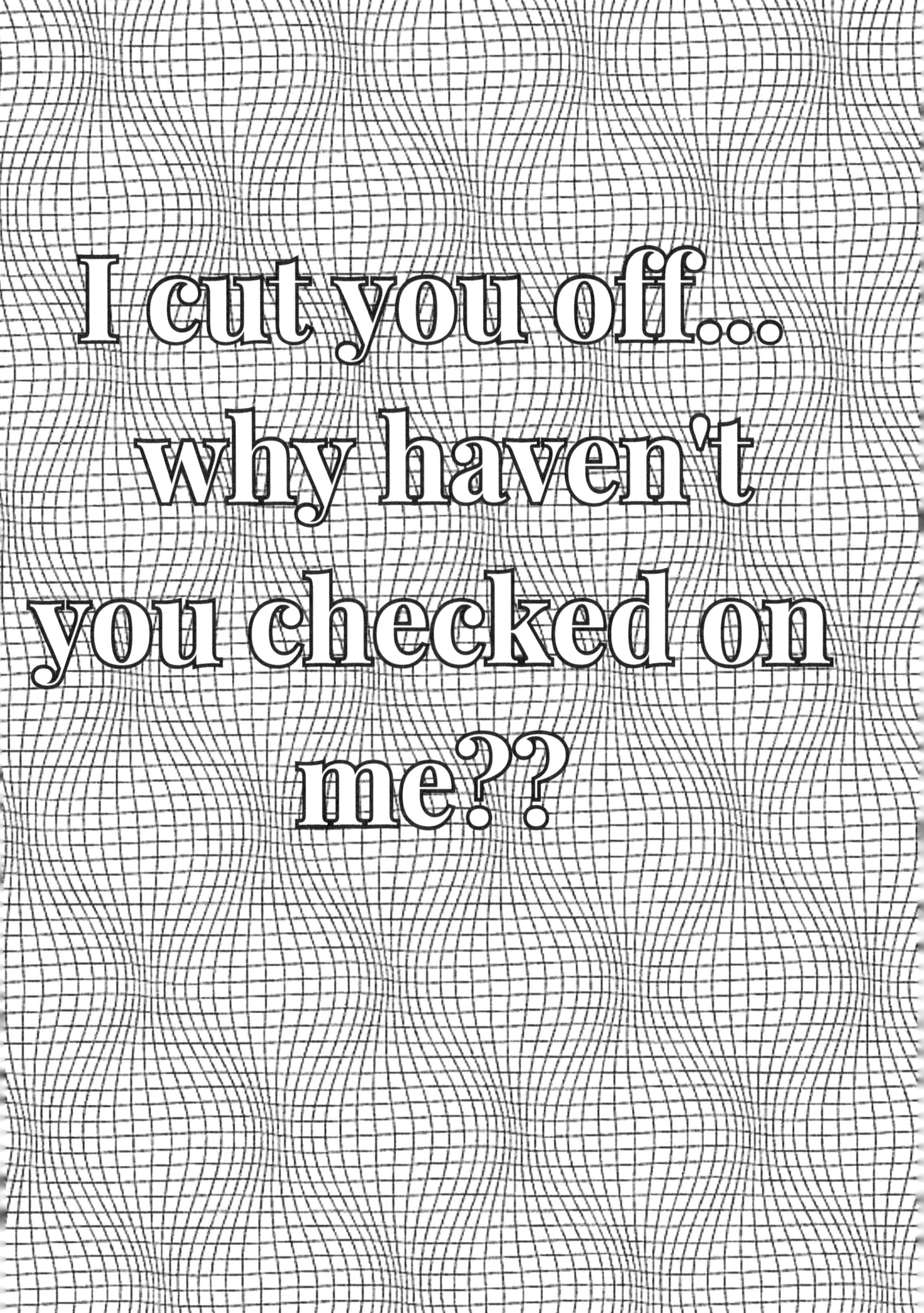

I cut you off...
why haven't
you checked on
me??

Sometimes sadness feels like the end.

Keep being
brave.

You were acting different...I noticed.

Rejection

HOW DARE YOU LOVE ME?

why can't
it all be
beginnings?
I'm good
at those.

Sensitive.

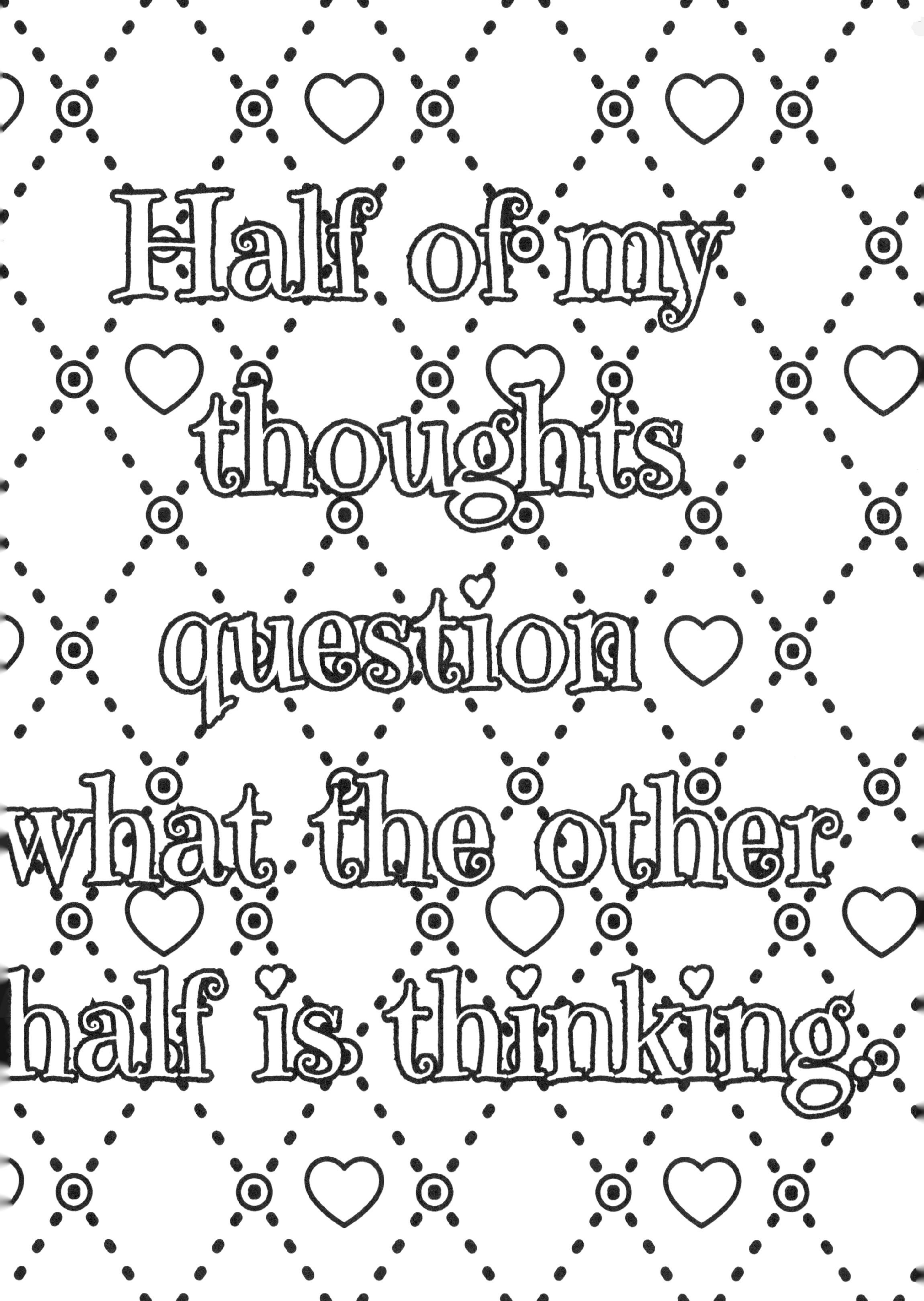

Half of my
thoughts
question
what the other
half is thinking.

Im fine,
but
not really.

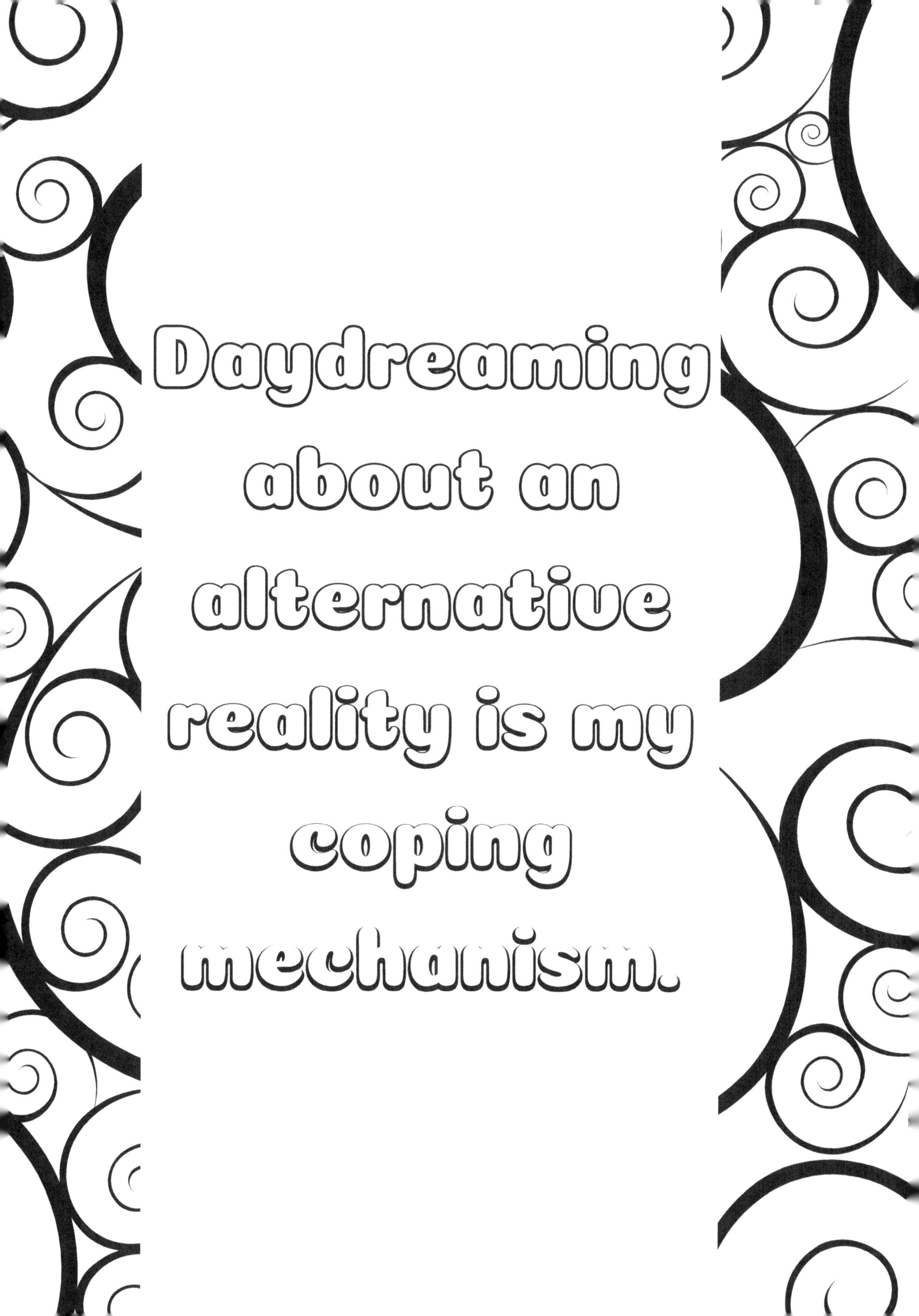

Daydreaming
about an
alternative
reality is my
coping
mechanism.

You

matter.

Thanks for

exsisting.